# These
# Are
# My
# Big
# Girl
# Pants

*Thank you to my family; my love
and gratitude for you lives beyond
the world of words.*

# These
# Are
# My
# Big
# Girl
# Pants

poetry and paintings on womanhood

## Amber Vittoria

Andrews McMeel
PUBLISHING®

## These Are My Big Girl Pants

Bright colors,
Vibrating patterns,
Flowers, and unicorns -
But don't worry,
My legs,
They are covered.

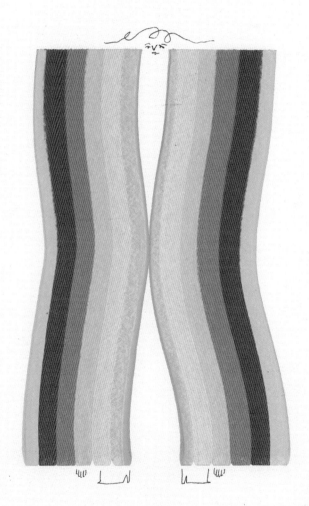

## Meanings of Flowers

I am sorry for your loss,
And I am happy for your growth.
I love you,
But I messed up.
These are your favorite,
For another trip around the sun.
A bouquet of emotions,
That although beautiful,
May not always be fun.

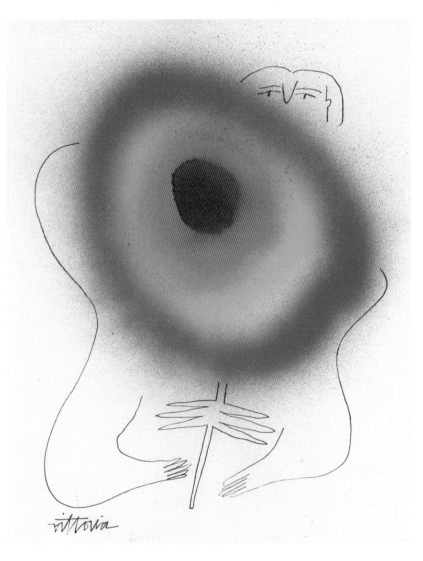

## Just Let Me Be Angry, Please

For a society that doesn't grant women the permission to outwardly feel emotions outside of pleasantries, a memoir.

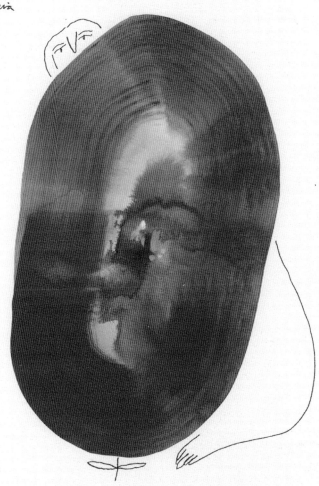

## The Beauty of Growth

That uncomfortable feeling,
Of the heavy shoulders,
The pang between the eyes,
That is you growing, my dear.
Similar to the soreness of your thigh,
And stretching of your bones,
Your emotional growth is something you feel,
And that is beautiful.

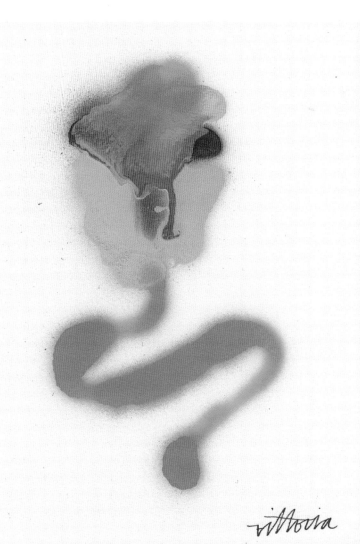

## Creating A Diamond

If you want to be a diamond, baby,
You need to survive the pressure.
Thank goodness, then,
That there are other things I'd rather be.

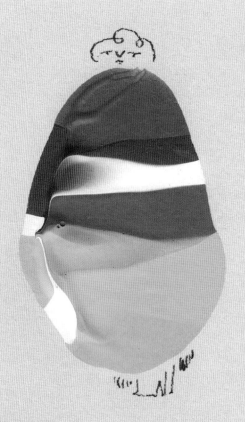

vittoria

## How I Viewed Myself

In the simpler times,
When my body could play,
And there was space in my mind.

I was young and strong,
My arms covered in dirt,
And my legs grew long.

My body was for me,
Running through sprinklers,
And I felt nothing but free.

## We Are Not The Same, Sadly

I read that to seek inspiration,
One man goes for solo walks at night.
How nice,
I wonder what that's like.

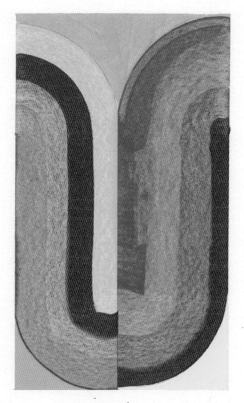

*vittoria*

## For a Momentary Escape, Call

If you're seeking a break,
Repeat this a few times:
Right now may be difficult,
But soon you'll be fine.

## Stretching Yourself

Is a good thing they say,
Until you're awake so long
That night turns back into day.

## Boxing Up My Sunshine

Locking up my joy,
Questioning my expertise,
Just because I'm not a boy.

vittoria

## Don't Let The Rage Out, Honey

They say it's never a good look,
To let out the rage,
But what a boring book,
To not pen anger to a page.

*vittoria*

## Making Sense of Nonsense

Here I go again,
Trying to find clarity
In the confusion,
A rarity.

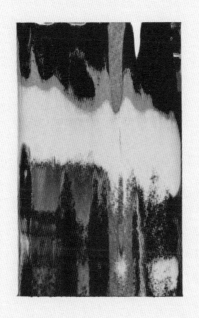

vittoria

## Tilt Your Head Left

And see the landscape;
Sometimes with an unexpected turn
A new perspective can take shape.

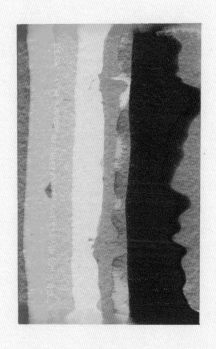

vittoria

## When Hunger And Rage Team Up

To envision sustenance
Success
So vividly,
My stomach growls.

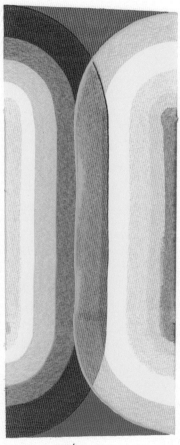

vittoria

## Not The Center of The Universe

Up for longer than the sun,
Witnessing our rise and fall
Around it, realizing we are
Just so small.

vittoria

## How It Must Flow

Pushing outwards towards my skin,
This is how my story begins?
They say when it is right, I'll know,
I suppose this is how it must go.

## Don't Interrupt My Internal Monologue

I said to myself,
As my thinking grew too loud
For my thinking.

## I Just Want To Bloom

In peace,
And instead of doing
The most for once,
I simply want
To do the least.

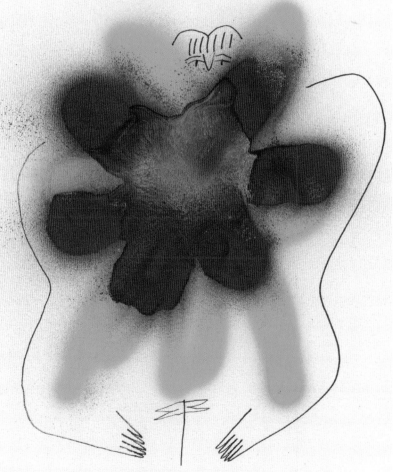

## These Are My Boundaries

Those who appreciate me
Will know no difference.

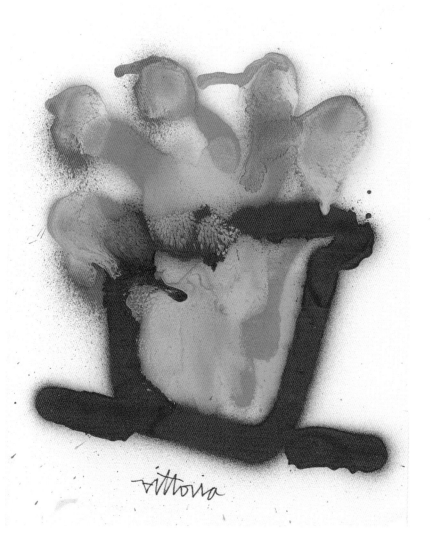

vittoria

## Time To Perform

For someone who
Cannot act,
I sure often find myself
Walking across a stage.

*vittoria*

## I Want To Dress Loud

And look you in the eye,
But please remember
That it's not an invitation
For you to try.

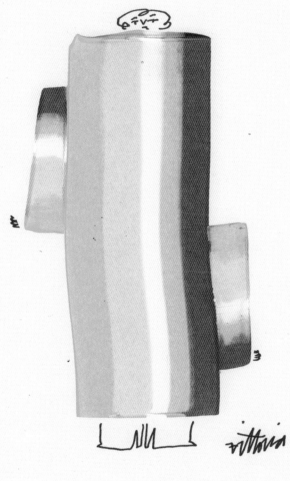

## Don't You Do Anything Else?

My breath is for me,
Please let my breadth be,
It's a decision I'll make myself.

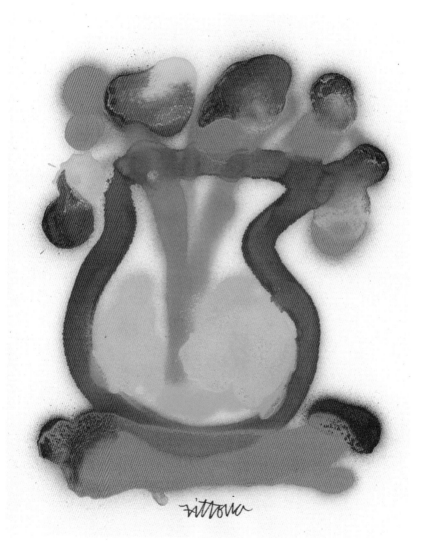

## I Talk To Me The Most

When I splits to we
In conversation,
I have to remind myself
To be more kind to me.

vittoria

## There Is More Than One Sun

To revolve yourself around;
When you're finished with one,
To another you can rebound.

vittoria

## The Queen Of Apathy

When there's a problem
You must float above,
Just remember,
The universe moves without you,
My love.

## I'm In My Own Head

Living rent free,
I'm trying to leave,
But how do I escape me?

*vittoria*

## Ridding Of The Itch

That builds in my mind.
The need to solve every situation,
Hinges on the hopes
That I'll one day be fine.

## Fixing My Gaze

Knowing I'm not here
To be looked at,
Frees me from the need
To constantly look at myself.

vittoria

## That's A Woman You Should Be

I'm simply trying to grow upwards,
And capture the sun,
Like a tree.
I don't want the approval
Of others,
Just me.

## I Can Do That

I'm glad this world
Affords you the opportunity
To do everything.
I wish I could say
The same.

*vittoria*

## I Don't Want To Rise With The Sun

For what happens
Behind my eyelids
Is the most fun.

vittoria

## Are We Done?

And by we I mean you;
I feel a boundary forming,
If only you knew.

*vittoria*

## When You See This Make A Wish

And instead of keeping it secret,
Throw it out into the universe
So fast you hear it swish.

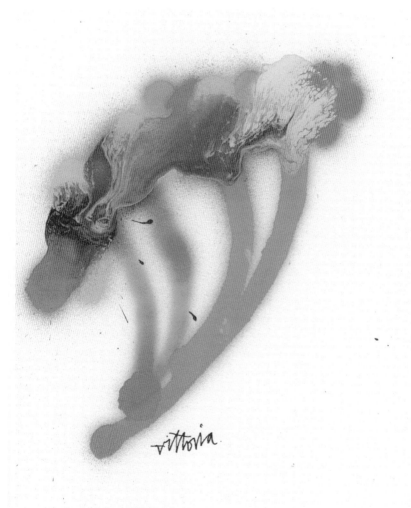

## Don't Nightmare, Dream

Unnecessary Preparation
Is to worry about
A narrow future yet lived;
Instead I'll try dreaming of
Bountiful times to come.

## When My Mind Thinks For Me

And my body is free,
The heights I'll reach
Like untethering a tree.

vittoria

## Inhaling The Future

And exhaling the past,
I wonder how long
My breathing will last.

vittoria

## When You're Outside A Cafe

Surrounded by folks
Speaking different languages,
And you do your best to embrace
The sound
Without the need to understand?
This is my relationship with happiness.

*vittoria*

## Blooming Beyond My Limits

Like vines bending away
From their wall,
I measure my success
In acquired minutes.

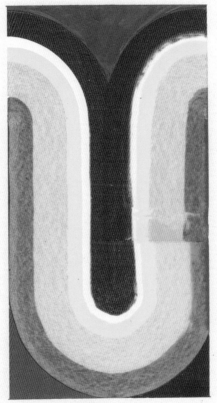

*vittoria*

## Self-Affirming

Take this moment
To say to yourself,
You are more than enough.
Come back as needed.

vittoria

## Alone In My Castle

While sitting on my throne,
All on my own,
Manifesting and contemplating
How much I've grown.

vittoria

## Is This Growth?

Reaching the top
Without my tippy toes,
I no longer need to choose
And can have both.

*vittoria*

## I Am Completely Okay

I am completely in sync.
I am completely at peace.
I am completely with it.
I am complete,
I think.

vittoria

## The Universe Can't BeBothered With Your Legacy

Time is running out,
Our fortunes fade to dust.
There isn't a legacy,
If there isn't an us.

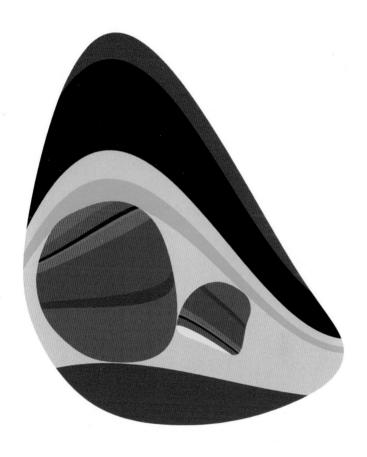

vittoria

## Oh, So Little

Do I care about
Your opinion
On my artwork,
Dear stranger.

*vittoria*

## Please Like Me

I say to myself,
As I look up towards the mirror.

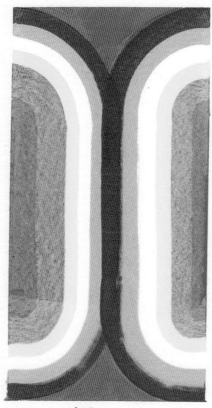

vittoria

## A Pimple And A Grey Hair

Stand closely to each other,
To remind me of how far I've come,
And How far I've yet to go.

## Capturing My Value

Is to capture my values,
And to remind myself
Time can't be overused.

vittoria

## We Are In This Together

Writing this between heartbeats,
Reminding myself this life is no small feat.
If you feel like this too,
Know I'm right there with you.

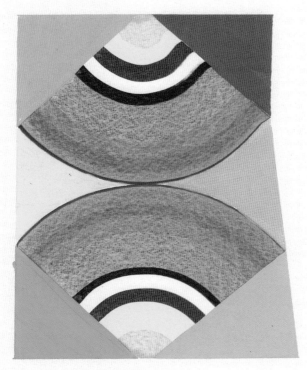

*vittoria*

## I'm Still Here

You do not need to see parts of me,
To know I am here.
The worry of not constantly being seen,
Is too damaging a fear.

vittoria

## Mental Marathon

My mind goes running,
As my feet stand still.
Why do I insist on training
Up these imaginary hills.

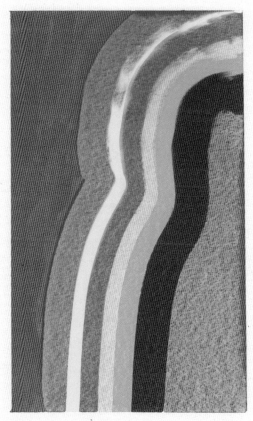

vittoria

## To Create Understanding

It is a tough task,
To hope when you share something
The other person just knows,
And doesn't have to ask.

vittoria

## I'm Not Striving For Perfection

I'm seeking honesty,
Though I'm finding myself unconsciously
Questioning my beauty.

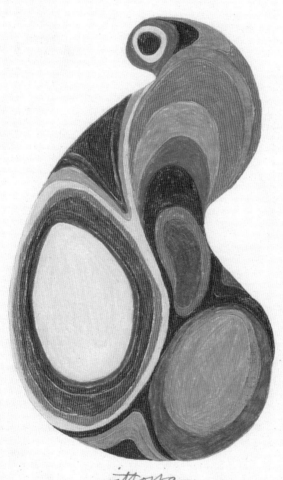

## If You Find This

While looking for a break,
I'm here to tell you
Close your eyes,
And breathe,
For your own sake.

## Leap With Me

Although my arc may not be perfect,
And my jump may end short,
If you're willing to take on the hurdle,
By the end you'll feel free.

vittoria

## I Live By The Hourglass

Even though I'm not shaped like one,
Our time is running out,
And I'd prefer to have fun.

## In My Dreams

My legs can paint,
And my hands can run;
I wouldn't need to know suffering,
In order to know fun.

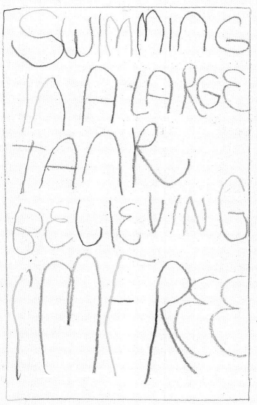

SWIMMING
IN A LARGE
TANK
BELIEVING
I'M FREE

vittoria

## I Remind Myself

Don't be mean
To the one person
You've never fully seen;
Even evergreens
Aren't evergreen.

vittoria

## The Wind Can Sing

If given the time,
Not everything will make sense,
Even if it rhymes.

vittoria

## When Heated In Battle

Remember the light
Could care less
If you're right.

## Why Does The World Hate Me?

I scream.
The universe is a rival to no one,
Echoes back the trees.

## Cool, Cool, Cool, Cool, Cool

The more I say it,
The more heated I become,
And if I explode,
I'll be blamed for the damage done.

vittoria

## Taking A Break

Is not lying awake,
Worrying about the mistakes you've yet to make,
Moving to wondering if you're a fake.
No, this is a sign you're about to break.

vittoria

## Whether In Fire

Or in ice,
It will all one day end;
Don't worry too much on
If you've done it right.

vittoria

## Here For The Sunset

Connecting to our past
And future selves
Who will experience
This feeling of conquering the sun
Yet another day.

## Cloudy With A Chance Of Rain

The rain patters on my window,
Little knocks on the door to my mind,
Kindly reminding me that without a drizzle,
I'd never appreciate the sunshine.

*vittoria*

## Welcome To The Unknown

A place where you can dream
Of happiness, joy, and flowers,
But instead I will end up
Worrying for hours.

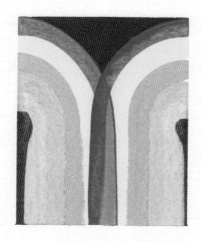

vittoria

## Falling Asleep With The Sun

You exist
And that is enough,
Soak the sun in, eyes closed.
It'll make life feel a bit less tough.

vittoria

## When The Sun Sees The Ground

A delicate dance
That color-soaks the sky,
(Insert here: our time, the one thing
We cannot hold onto, but try)
Happening twice a day,
To say hello and goodbye.

vittoria

## Look Ma, No Hands

With the training wheels
Bent upwards,
I raise my hands to the sky,
Realizing I now fully trust myself.

vettova

Andrews McMeel Publishing
a division of Andrews McMeel Universal
1130 Walnut Street, Kansas City, Missouri 64106

www.andrewsmcmeel.com

23 24 25 26 27 TEN 10 9 8 7 6 5 4 3 2 1

ISBN: 978-1-5248-7578-7

Library of Congress Control Number: 2022941126

Editor: Patty Rice
Art Director: Tiffany Meairs
Production Editor: Brianna Westervelt
Production Manager: Shona Burns